AF231122

Word of Life

Sermon Notebook
for Women

By
Word Span Publishing, Inc.

Word of Life:
Sermon Notebook for Women

Copyright © 2023 Word Span Publishing, Inc.

All rights reserved.

ISBN: 978-1-961095-02-1

The
Word of Life

"For the word of God is living and active. Sharper than any double-edged sword, it penetrates even to dividing soul and spirit, joints and marrow; it judges the thoughts and attitudes of the heart."

Hebrew 4:12

The Holy Bible, New International Version

Date:

Speaker:

Topic:

Scripture References:

Notes:

Key Points:

Thoughts & Reflections:

Prayer Request:

Date: Speaker:

Topic:

Scripture References:

Notes:
____

____

____

____

____

____

____

____

Key Points:

Thoughts & Reflections:

Prayer Request:

Date:

Speaker:

Topic:

Scripture References:

Notes:

Key Points:

____

____

____

____

____

____

____

Thoughts & Reflections:

Prayer Request:

| Date: | Speaker: |

| Topic: |

Scripture References:

Notes:
____

____

____

____

____

____

____

____

____

____

Key Points:

Thoughts & Reflections:

Prayer Request:

Date: Speaker:

Topic:

Scripture References:

Notes:

____

____

____

____

____

____

____

____

____

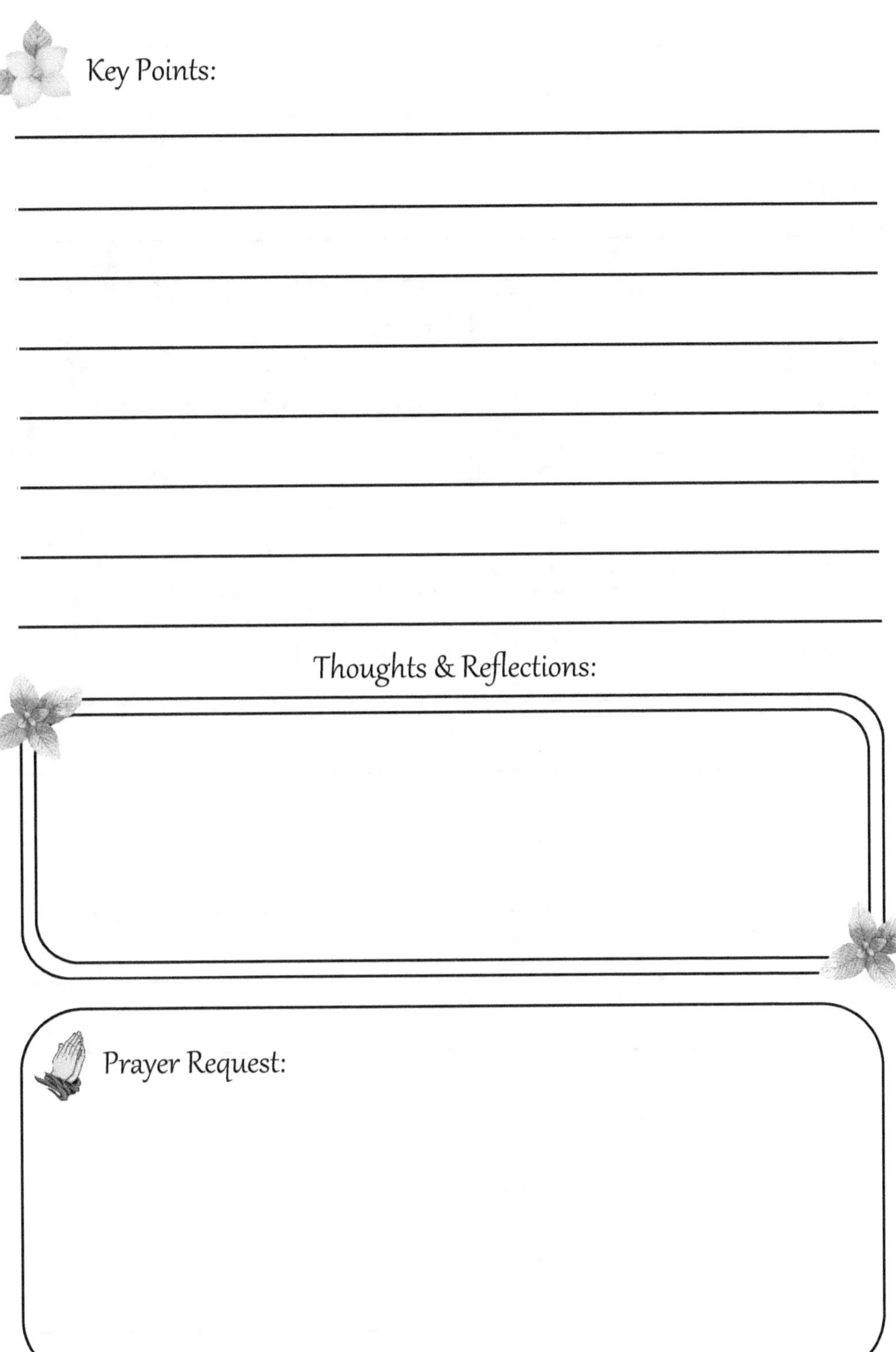

Key Points:

Thoughts & Reflections:

Prayer Request:

Date:

Speaker:

Topic:

Scripture References:

Notes:

Key Points:

Thoughts & Reflections:

Prayer Request:

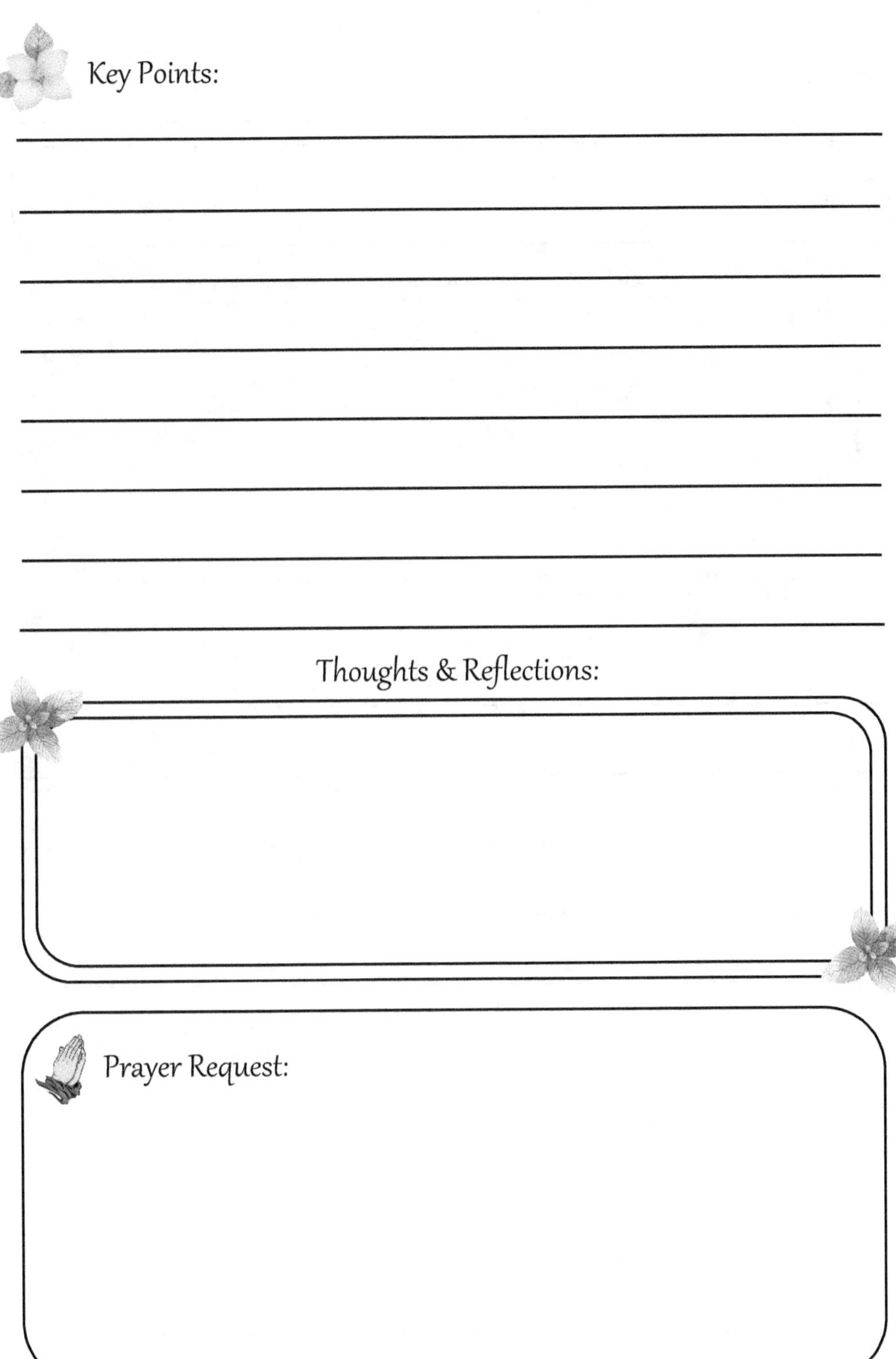

Date:

Speaker:

Topic:

Scripture References:

Notes:

Key Points:

Thoughts & Reflections:

Prayer Request:

Date: | Speaker:

Topic:

Scripture References:

Notes:

____

____

____

____

____

____

____

____

____

Key Points:

Thoughts & Reflections:

Prayer Request:

Date:

Speaker:

Topic:

Scripture References:

Notes:

Key Points:

Thoughts & Reflections:

Prayer Request:

Date:

Speaker:

Topic:

Scripture References:

Notes:

Key Points:

Thoughts & Reflections:

Prayer Request:

Date:

Speaker:

Topic:

Scripture References:

Notes:

Key Points:

____

____

____

____

____

____

____

____

Thoughts & Reflections:

Prayer Request:

Date:

Speaker:

Topic:

Scripture References:

Notes:

Key Points:

____
____
____
____
____
____
____
____

Thoughts & Reflections:

Prayer Request:

Date:

Speaker:

Topic:

Scripture References:

Notes:
____

____

____

____

____

____

____

____

____

Key Points:

Thoughts & Reflections:

Prayer Request:

| Date: | Speaker: |

| Topic: |

Scripture References:

Notes:
____

____

____

____

____

____

____

____

Key Points:

Thoughts & Reflections:

Prayer Request:

Date:

Speaker:

Topic:

Scripture References:

Notes:

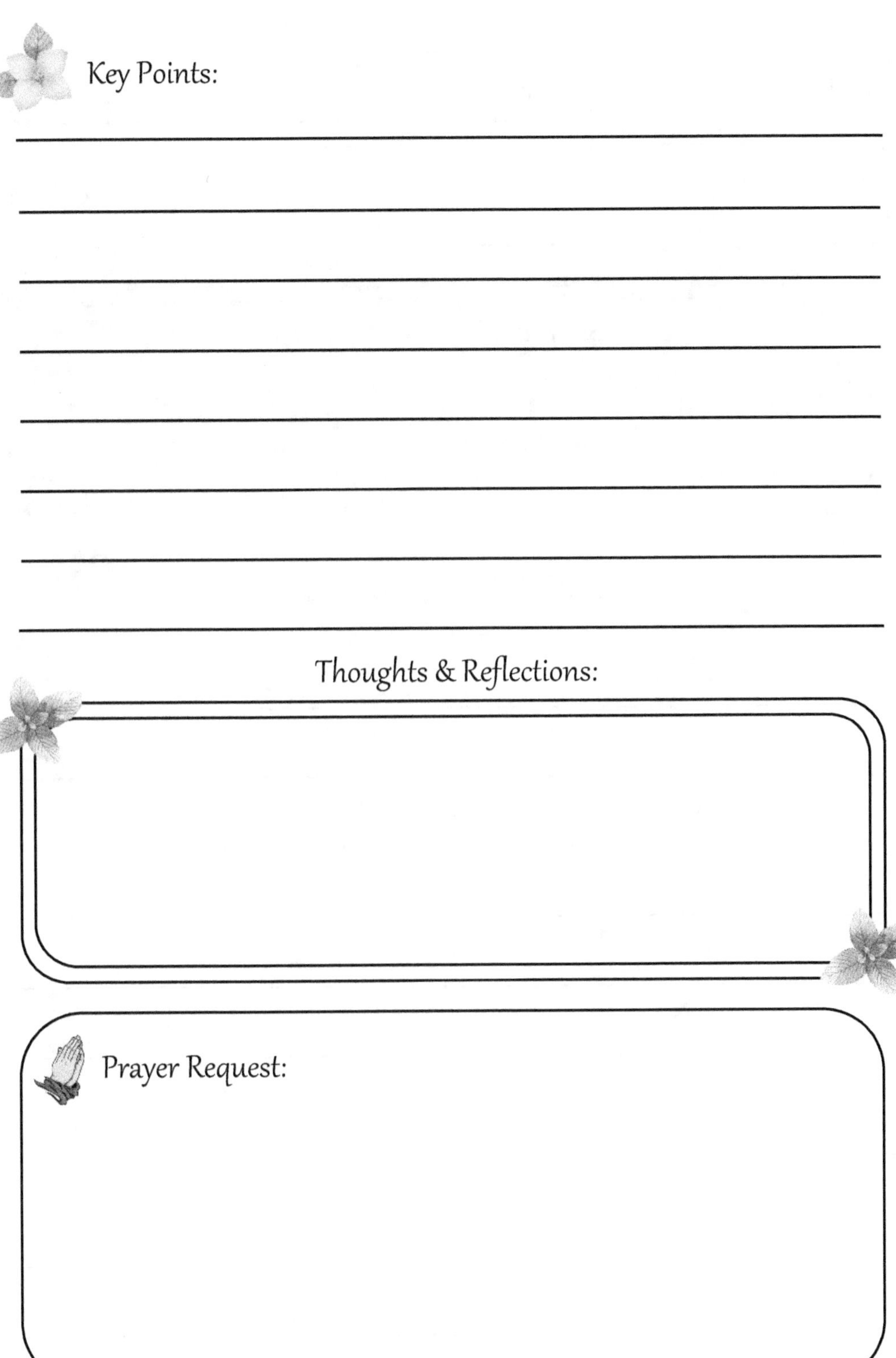

Key Points:

____

____

____

____

____

____

____

Thoughts & Reflections:

Prayer Request:

Date:

Speaker:

Topic:

Scripture References:

Notes:

Key Points:

____

____

____

____

____

____

____

Thoughts & Reflections:

Prayer Request:

Date:

Speaker:

Topic:

Scripture References:

Notes:

Key Points:

Thoughts & Reflections:

Prayer Request:

Date:

Speaker:

Topic:

Scripture References:

Notes:
____

____

____

____

____

____

____

____

____

Key Points:

Thoughts & Reflections:

Prayer Request:

Date:

Speaker:

Topic:

Scripture References:

Notes:

Key Points:

____

____

____

____

____

____

____

Thoughts & Reflections:

Prayer Request:

<table>
<tr><td>Date:</td><td>Speaker:</td></tr>
</table>

Topic:

Scripture References:

Notes:

____

____

____

____

____

____

____

____

____

____

Key Points:

Thoughts & Reflections:

Prayer Request:

Date: Speaker:

Topic:

Scripture References:

Notes:

____

____

____

____

____

____

____

____

____

Key Points:

Thoughts & Reflections:

Prayer Request:

Date:

Speaker:

Topic:

Scripture References:

Notes:

Key Points:

Thoughts & Reflections:

Prayer Request:

Date:

Speaker:

Topic:

Scripture References:

Notes:

Key Points:

Thoughts & Reflections:

Prayer Request:

Date:

Speaker:

Topic:

Scripture References:

Notes:

____

____

____

____

____

____

____

____

____

Key Points:

Thoughts & Reflections:

Prayer Request:

Date:

Speaker:

Topic:

Scripture References:

Notes:

Key Points:

Thoughts & Reflections:

Prayer Request:

Date:

Speaker:

Topic:

Scripture References:

Notes:

____

____

____

____

____

____

____

____

____

Key Points:

Thoughts & Reflections:

Prayer Request:

Date:

Speaker:

Topic:

Scripture References:

Notes:

Key Points:

Thoughts & Reflections:

Prayer Request:

Date:

Speaker:

Topic:

Scripture References:

Notes:

____

____

____

____

____

____

____

____

____

Key Points:

Thoughts & Reflections:

Prayer Request:

Date:

Speaker:

Topic:

Scripture References:

Notes:

____

____

____

____

____

____

____

____

____

Key Points:

Thoughts & Reflections:

Prayer Request:

Date:

Speaker:

Topic:

Scripture References:

Notes:

Key Points:

Thoughts & Reflections:

Prayer Request:

Date:

Speaker:

Topic:

Scripture References:

Notes:

Key Points:

____

____

____

____

____

____

Thoughts & Reflections:

Prayer Request:

| Date: | Speaker: |

Topic:

Scripture References:

Notes:
____
____
____
____
____
____
____
____
____

Key Points:

Thoughts & Reflections:

Prayer Request:

Date:

Speaker:

Topic:

Scripture References:

Notes:
____

____

____

____

____

____

____

____

____

____

Key Points:

Thoughts & Reflections:

Prayer Request:

| Date: | Speaker: |

| Topic: |

Scripture References:

Notes:

____

____

____

____

____

____

____

____

____

____

Key Points:

Thoughts & Reflections:

Prayer Request:

<table><tr><td>Date:</td><td>Speaker:</td></tr></table>

Topic:

Scripture References:

Notes:

____

____

____

____

____

____

____

____

____

Key Points:

Thoughts & Reflections:

Prayer Request:

Date:

Speaker:

Topic:

Scripture References:

Notes:

____

____

____

____

____

____

____

____

____

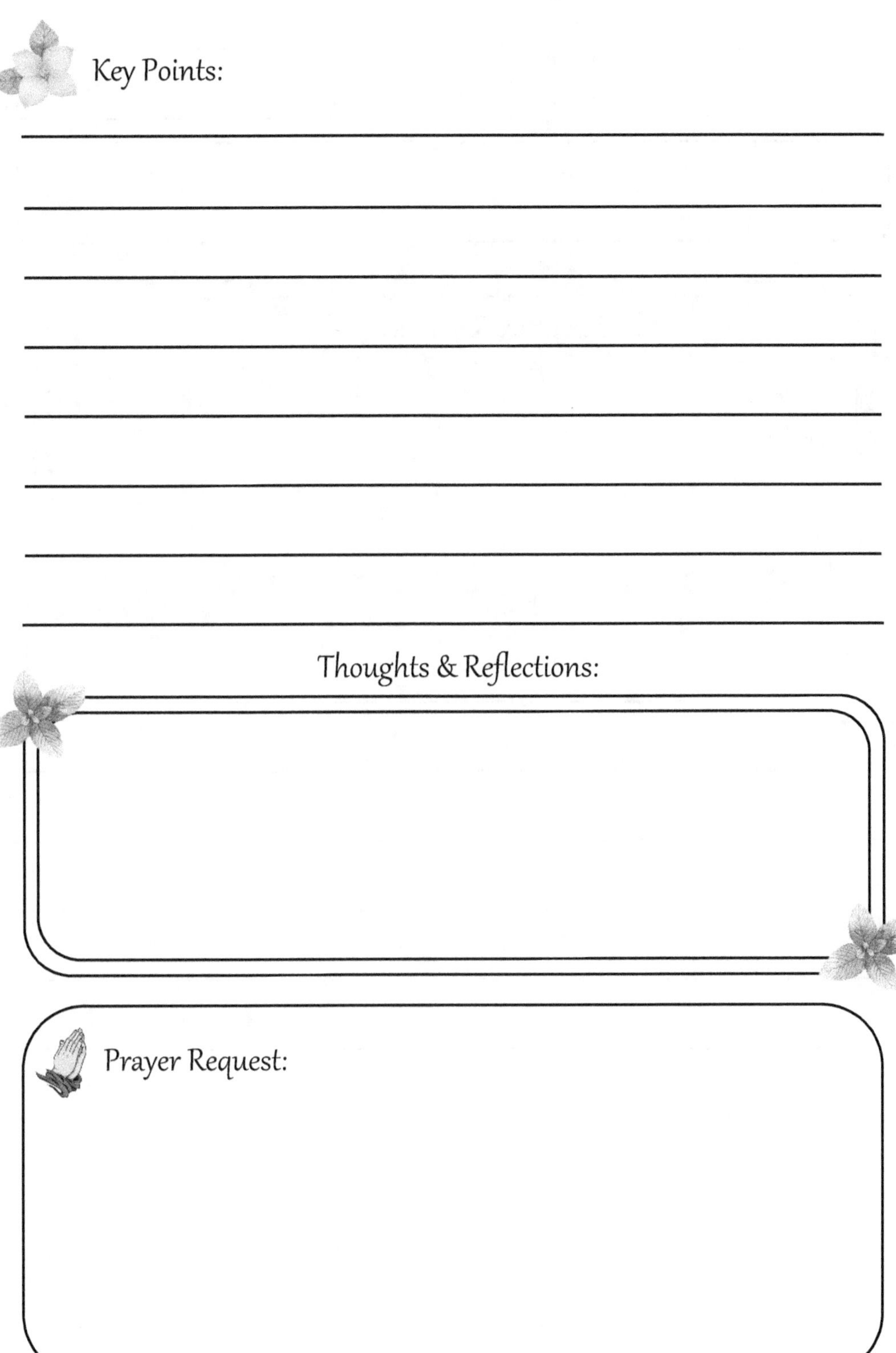

Key Points:

Thoughts & Reflections:

Prayer Request:

Date:

Speaker:

Topic:

Scripture References:

Notes:

Key Points:

Thoughts & Reflections:

Prayer Request:

| Date: | Speaker: |

| Topic: |

Scripture References:

Notes:

____

____

____

____

____

____

____

____

Key Points:

Thoughts & Reflections:

Prayer Request:

Date: Speaker:

Topic:

Scripture References:

____

____

____

____

____

____

____

____

____

____

____

Key Points:

Thoughts & Reflections:

Prayer Request:

| Date: | Speaker: |

| Topic: |

Scripture References:

Notes:

____

____

____

____

____

____

____

____

____

Key Points:

____

____

____

____

____

____

____

Thoughts & Reflections:

Prayer Request:

Date:

Speaker:

Topic:

Scripture References:

Notes:

____

____

____

____

____

____

____

____

____

Key Points:

Thoughts & Reflections:

Prayer Request:

Date: Speaker:

Topic:

Scripture References:

Notes:

____

____

____

____

____

____

____

____

____

Key Points:

Thoughts & Reflections:

Prayer Request:

Date:

Speaker:

Topic:

Scripture References:

Notes:

Key Points:

Thoughts & Reflections:

Prayer Request:

Date:

Speaker:

Topic:

Scripture References:

Notes:

Key Points:

Thoughts & Reflections:

Prayer Request:

Date:

Speaker:

Topic:

Scripture References:

Notes:

Key Points:

Thoughts & Reflections:

Prayer Request:

Date:

Speaker:

Topic:

Scripture References:

Notes:

Key Points:

____
____
____
____
____
____
____

Thoughts & Reflections:

Prayer Request:

| Date: | Speaker: |

| Topic: |

Scripture References:

Notes:

____

____

____

____

____

____

____

____

____

Key Points:

Thoughts & Reflections:

Prayer Request:

| Date: | Speaker: |

Topic:

Scripture References:

Notes:

____

____

____

____

____

____

____

____

____

____

Key Points:

Thoughts & Reflections:

Prayer Request:

Date:

Speaker:

Topic:

Scripture References:

Notes:

Key Points:

Thoughts & Reflections:

Prayer Request:

| Date: | Speaker: |

| Topic: |

Scripture References:

Notes:
____
____
____
____
____
____
____
____
____

Key Points:

Thoughts & Reflections:

Prayer Request:

Date:

Speaker:

Topic:

Scripture References:

Notes:

Key Points:

____

____

____

____

____

____

Thoughts & Reflections:

Prayer Request:

| Date: | Speaker: |

| Topic: |

Scripture References:

Key Points:

Thoughts & Reflections:

Prayer Request:

God Bless!

Please take a quick moment to review this book and show your support for independent publishers.

Thank You!